GET INFORMED—STAY INFORMED

International Alliances and Treaties

Natalie Hyde

A Crabtree Forest Book

Crabtree Publishing
crabtreebooks.com

Crabtree Publishing

crabtreebooks.com 800-387-7650

 In Canada: We acknowledge the financial support of the Government of Canada through the Canada Book Fund for our publishing activities.

Author: Natalie Hyde
Series research and development: Reagan Miller
Editor-in-chief: Kathy Middleton
Editors: Ellen Rodger, Janine Deschenes
Proofreader: Wendy Scavuzzo
Project coordinator: Melissa Boyce
Graphic design: Katherine Berti
Photo research: Natalie Hyde, Katherine Berti

Hardcover 978-1-0398-1517-9
Paperback 978-1-0398-1543-8
Ebook (pdf) 978-1-0398-1595-7
Epub 978-1-0398-1569-8

Printed in the U.S.A./072023/CG20230214

Library and Archives Canada Cataloguing in Publication

Available at Library and Archives Canada

Library of Congress Cataloging-in-Publication Data

Available at the Library of Congress

Published in Canada
Crabtree Publishing
616 Welland Avenue
St. Catharines, Ontario
L2M 5V6

Published in the United States
Crabtree Publishing
347 Fifth Avenue
Suite 1402-145
New York, NY 10016

Photographs and reproductions:
Alamy Stock Photo
RBM Vintage Images: p. 19
iStock by Getty Images
Bet_Noire: p. 41
viper-zero: p. 15 (top)
zmeel: p. 13
National Archives, U.S. Government. 3:4:1789: p. 10
Shutterstock
CameraCraft: p. 29
Captain Wang: p. 37 (bottom)
catastrophe_OL: p. 25
ChameleonsEye: p. 15 (bottom)
eskystudio: p. 11
JessicaGirvan: p. 39
noamgali: p. 8
Northfoto: p. 28
paparazzza: p. 35
Ringo Chiu: p. 32–33
Ryan Boedi: p. 22–23 (top)
Yau Ming Low: p. 34
Wikimedia Commons
Adam sk~commonswiki: p. 4 (top right)
Library of Congress, Reproduction number LC-USW33-019093-C: p. 4 (center left)
DOD photo by U.S. Air Force Master Sgt. Jerry Morrison: p. 5 (top)
Firdavs Kulolov: p. 21 (top)
Flickr user Michael Foran—: p. 21 (bottom)
Henry Mühlpfordt: p. 22 (bottom)
Master Uegly: p. 31 (top)
National Archives and Records Administration, NAID 195617: p. 17 (bottom)
RaviC: p. 37 (top)
The New York Times 1 (May 8, 1915). "Lusitania Sunk by a Submarine, Probably 1,260 Dead": p. 16
UK Ministry of Defence: p. 31 (bottom)
US Government: p. 9
White House: p. 36
www.propublica.org
Screen Shot 2022-11-15 at 12.00.08 PM: p. 12 (left inset)
www.snopes.com
Screen Shot 2022-11-15 at 11.58.10 AM: p. 12 (right inset)
All other images by Shutterstock
Diagrams: Katherine Berti

CONTENTS

1 WHY WE MAKE ALLIANCES

It's good to have a friend in a fight. This is true whether you are an individual or an entire country. Since the earliest times, countries have agreed to work together for their **mutual benefit** and protection. Rulers of smaller nations or regions joined forces to defeat a common enemy. Trade agreements go back thousands of years, as well.

MODERN TRADE

Contemporary trade agreements involve more than a handshake and the swap of goods or coin. They evolve over time. The Cobden-Chevalier **Treaty** is often called the first free trade agreement. It was signed in 1860 between Great Britain and France. The treaty allowed goods, such as wine and silk from France, to be traded for coal and iron from Great Britain without trade taxes called "tariffs."

> *There is only one thing worse than fighting with allies, and that is fighting without them.*
>
> Winston Churchill

▼ Ancient civilizations sent traders and **envoys** to buy and sell trade items such as incense, silk, and spices. The ancient city of Petra, in modern-day Jordan, became the center of a trade empire more than 2,000 years ago.

▲ The North Atlantic Treaty Organization (NATO) headquarters is in Brussels, Belgium. There, representatives meet to discuss the freedom and security of member nations.

QUESTIONS TO ASK

Within this book are three types of boxes with questions to help your critical thinking about international alliances and treaties. The icons will help you identify them.

THE CENTRAL ISSUES

Learning about the main points of information.

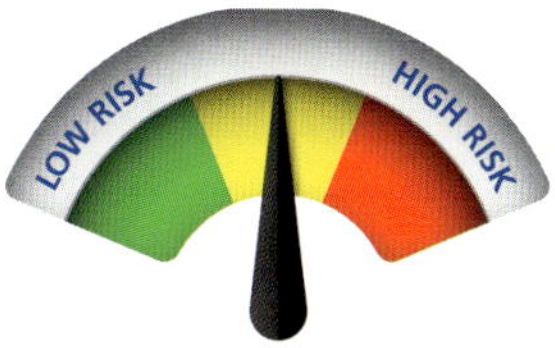

WHAT'S AT STAKE

Helping you determine how the issue will affect you.

ASK YOUR OWN QUESTIONS

Prompts to address gaps in your understanding.

TREATIES TODAY

Today, there are more than 560 treaties between two or more nations. Modern treaties and alliances cover a broad range of matters such as human rights, trade, **disarmament**, security alliances, and protection of the environment. A treaty is a formal agreement or arrangement created between two or more countries or their leaders. An alliance is a union or relationship in which people, groups, or countries agree to work together.

POWER AND IMPACT

Treaties and alliances are important because they have been used to end wars, settle land disputes, and increase the wealth of countries. Your personal life is affected by the treaties or alliances your country or community has agreed to. These agreements mean militaries might be called to fight, or prices for goods and services might be tied to another country's economy. These treaties can also affect freedoms, safety, and business opportunities.

WHY STAY INFORMED?

The agreements between nations are not **permanent**. Treaties and alliances can be created, broken, long lasting, or short-lived. New leaders, new governments, and world events can all result in new treaties and alliances or the end of old ones. Over time, the number of alliances has increased. At the same time, the number of wars between nations has dropped dramatically. This is likely due to the stable balance of power created by these alliances.

A CHANGING TOPIC

Because the number of treaties and alliances is constantly changing, it is important to have accurate and up-to-date information. By keeping up to date, we can better understand what is happening in the world and how events will affect our lives. Treaties and alliances are a global topic. That means the information we need will be found in many different places. It also means there will be many points of view. Different **stakeholders** might have different opinions on whether the alliance or treaty is **beneficial**.

▼ This ancient treaty is written on a clay tablet. It is a peace treaty between the Egyptians and Hittites in 1300–1200 B.C.E.

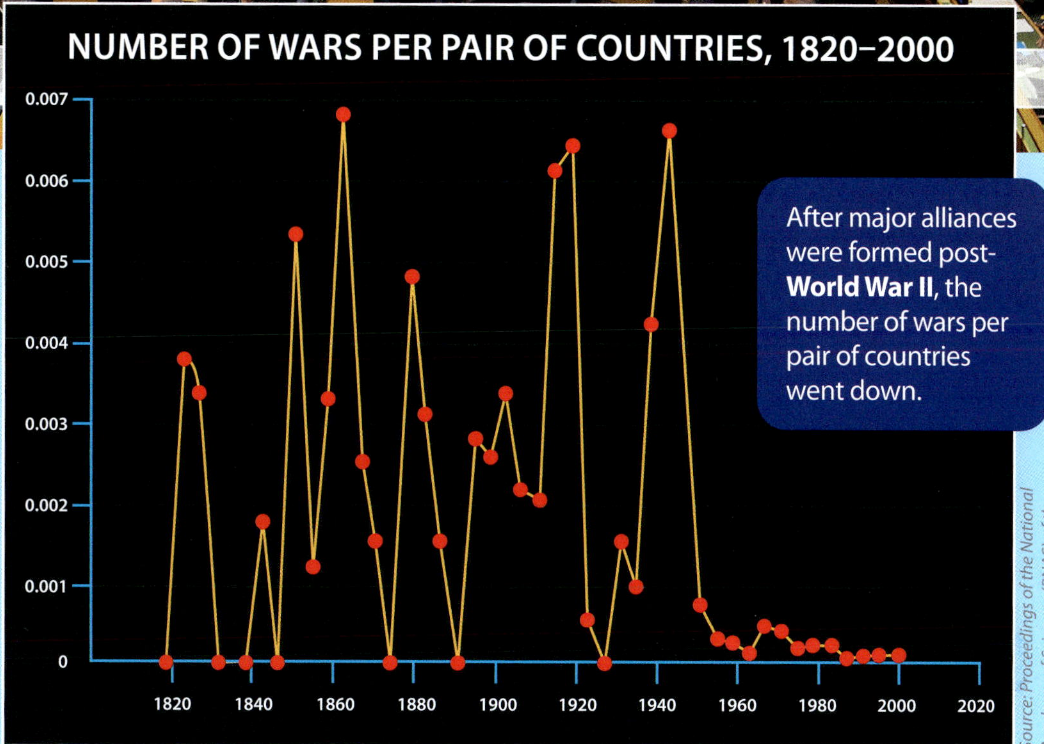

Source: Proceedings of the National Academy of Sciences (PNAS) of the United States of America, 2015

STAYING UP TO DATE

Understanding what an international treaty or alliance does is important. But it is just as important to understand that as new alliances and treaties are created and altered, or as old ones end, things might change in your life, community, or country. This can help you figure out such things as where it is safe to travel, what goods to buy, the business opportunities that might come along, or the steps you might need to take to protect yourself and your family.

This book will start by exploring where to find accurate and up-to-date information on international treaties and alliances. It will look at the different kinds of agreements and how they have helped shape our world. Then it will also help you devise a plan to keep yourself informed as the subject changes.

2 HOW TO GET INFORMED

Treaties and alliances are complicated issues. They are created only after a long process in which every detail is examined to make sure one side will not have an unfair advantage over the other. The goal of any international agreement is for both sides to benefit. Once an international treaty or alliance is signed, it can have far-reaching consequences.

LEADERS AND ORGANIZATIONS

For any topic, it is important to figure out who the key players are, learn the background and history, and be able to use and understand the vocabulary of the topic. Key players in alliances and treaties are the leaders of the groups or nations that have the power to create, sign, and enforce them. Key players are also the organizations that oversee alliances to make sure all the members are following the guidelines written into the contract.

> *"We've got to be moving together, working together, leading the country together and ensuring that we achieve the objectives that our alliance has set out for itself."*
>
> Cyril Ramaphosa, fifth president of South Africa

▲ An accord is another name for an official treaty or agreement. The Abraham Accords were signed in 2020 by Israel, the United Arab Emirates, and Bahrain at the White House in Washington. These were agreements to establish **diplomatic relations** between these countries.

▲ In 1945, British Prime Minister Clement Attlee, American President Harry S. Truman, and Soviet leader Joseph Stalin signed the Potsdam Agreement. It was a plan for peace and the treatment of Germany after World War II.

WHAT LEADS TO TREATIES?

Background about international alliances and treaties includes the history of countries who enter into agreements. What were the events, conflicts, and natural disasters that may have led to them signing trade, security, or environmental agreements? Alliances are often a **strategic** move to protect a nation and its people and resources.

TREATY TERMINOLOGY

Being familiar with topic-specific vocabulary will give you a better understanding of the information you might find. For example, the word "accession" means that a state accepts the opportunity to join a treaty signed and **negotiated** by other states. Knowing the difference between a "bilateral treaty" (agreement between two states or nations) and a "multilateral treaty" (agreement between three or more) will help you grasp the significance of what you are reading.

THE CENTRAL ISSUES

Does the balance of power created by international alliances make the world safer from conflict?

When you are looking to get informed, you first need to turn to source material. Source material is anything created to provide information. It can be primary, secondary, or tertiary (see sidebar on opposite page). Source material can be written, spoken, audio, or visual. Written sources include documents, articles, reports, or studies. Spoken and audio sources might be interviews, music lyrics, speeches, or recordings. Visual material includes things you can see, such as illustrations, posters, artwork, buildings, or sculptures.

Source material can be found in many places. Libraries, archives, museums, and government offices all retain documents, photos, and **artifacts**. The Internet is a storehouse of all kinds of data. Studies, research, reports from organizations, statistics from governments, and news articles are all available online.

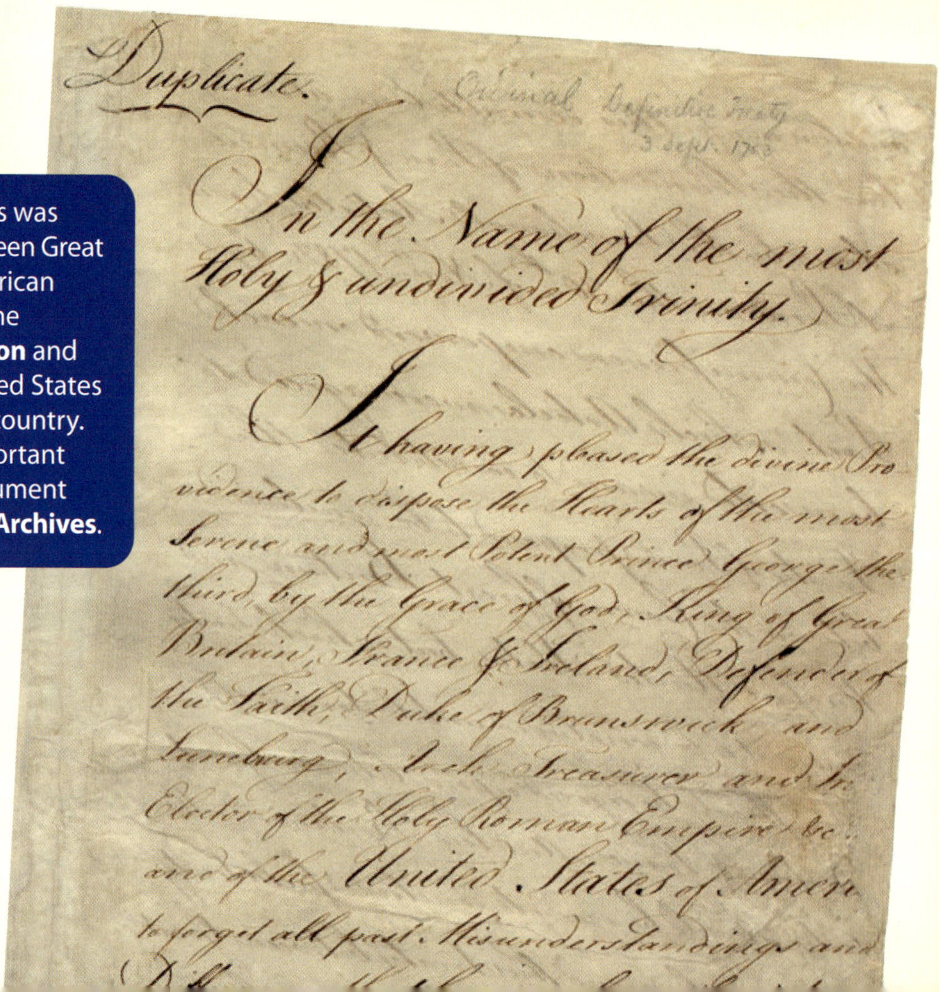
Duplicate.
In the Name of the most
Holy & undivided Trinity.
It having pleased the divine Pro
vidence to dispose the Hearts of the most
Serene and most Potent Prince George the
third, by the Grace of God, King of Great
Britain, France & Ireland, Defender of
the Faith, Duke of Brunswick and
Lunebourg, Arch Treasurer and Pr
Elector of the Holy Roman Empire &c.
and of the United States of Ameri
to forget all past Misunderstandings and

▶ The Treaty of Paris was signed in 1783 between Great Britain and the American Colonies. It ended the **American Revolution** and recognized the United States as an independent country. The treaty is an important primary source document kept at the National **Archives**.

RECOGNIZING BIAS

Sometimes information is slanted, or presented from an angle that favors one point of view. This is called "bias." Bias can be intentional or unintentional. It is not necessarily a negative thing, but it is important to recognize it. If the bias in a source is known, you can interpret what you read, knowing you may have to account for it when drawing your own conclusions.

When it comes to international treaties and alliances, different countries have different viewpoints on how well a treaty or alliance is working, or what problems may exist. These viewpoints can create bias in how information, such as the efficacy of an alliance, is presented by one country versus another. Understanding that there may be different viewpoints on the same treaty or alliance is key to forming a balanced opinion.

KEY INFORMATION

Primary sources are the original creators or owners of information. A military leader's report on a conflict is one example.

Secondary sources are reports, analyses, and interpretations of primary sources. A magazine article about the effects of a free trade agreement is a secondary source.

Tertiary sources are summaries or databases of primary and secondary information. They include Wikipedia articles or entries in encyclopedias.

▼ Not all information has been digitally copied. The Library of Congress in Washington, DC, is the largest library in the world and houses a huge amount of physical source material.

It is important to remember that not all data found either in print or digitally is equally reliable. It is vital to check where, how, why, and by whom the information was created. Misinformation and fake news clog our information highways. It is vital to figure out what data can be relied upon and what should be **discarded**.

EXPERTS AND EXPERTISE

Treaties and alliances are mostly between different nations. This can include **Indigenous** nations living within a country or **territory**. Some countries have limitations on their news reports and this can affect how information is presented. Experts from around the world can also give their expertise on the subject.

Checking the **credentials** of authors of studies, articles, or websites is vital. People sometimes claim they are experts on a topic, but do not have the needed education or support from scientists in that field. Organizations often have a mission statement. This means information on their websites or in their documents is biased to support these views and goals. This bias has to be taken into consideration when using their data in forming an opinion.

▼ A news outlet or website is more likely to be reliable when it lists its sources at the end of an article or under a photo. You can check these sources to find out whether what is being reported is true. Sources used for this book are listed on page 46.

▼ Some websites, such as Snopes, are dedicated to fact-checking. They look at sources to try to verify whether widely-reported stories are true.

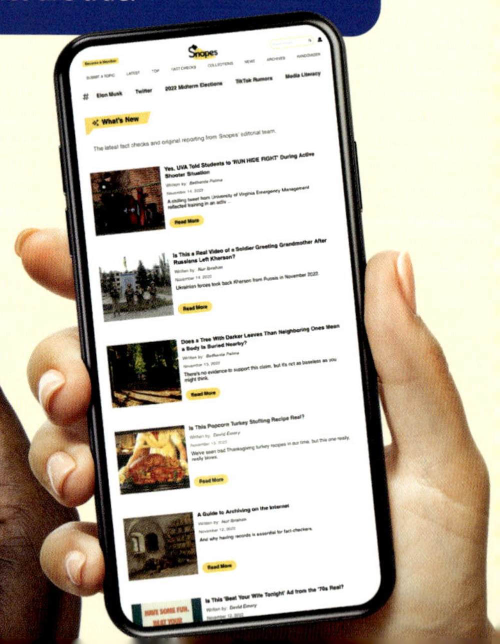

TIME AND PLACE RULE

Finding and judging which information is reliable can be difficult. The Time and Place Rule can help with figuring this out. It states that the closer in time and place a source and its creator were to an event, the more reliable the source will be. That is because facts and details are often lost or misremembered over time. An interview conducted just after a world war will give a much more accurate account of how the event affected people than the same questions asked 10 years later.

ASK YOUR OWN QUESTIONS

To determine if a source is credible, consider:

- Does the creator have solid credentials and expertise in the topic?
- Does the headline match the story?
- Is the publisher known to be reliable?
- What sources did the creator use?
- Is the source relevant and up to date?
- Is the source meant to be a joke or clickbait?

▼ Some people believe free access information websites, such as Wikipedia, are less trustworthy because they allow users to create or edit articles. Over the years, Wikipedia has improved its policies to ensure more accuracy in articles. As with any website, it is important to double check details with other sources.

3 INTERNATIONAL TREATIES AND ALLIANCES

There are many reasons why international treaties and alliances are created. Security alliances are put in place to keep nations safe from war, conflict, and **terrorism**. Trade alliances help economies by reducing tariffs, or taxes, on goods and services that are exchanged between countries. Some treaties are put in place to tackle problems that affect the whole world, such as climate change and human rights violations.

TREATIES AS TOOLS

By the 1900s, treaties and alliances were commonly used and created. International treaties and alliances are vital to keep a balance of power in the world. When that balance tips, global peace and human rights can be put at risk. The United States (U.S.) enters into more than 200 treaties and other international agreements per year.

> “*Good alliances are made of strong, capable partners.*”
>
> American politician and former U.S. Secretary of Defense, Mark Esper

EARLY TREATIES

One of the earliest examples of a treaty was a border agreement made around 3100 B.C.E. between two city-states in Sumer (modern day Iraq). From the 1400s, almost all major civilizations had entered into some form of international treaty or alliance.

With exploration and **colonization** happening throughout the 1800s, many international treaties were created between European colonizers and Indigenous peoples. However, many of these treaties over land use, rights, and trade alliances were broken. Colonizing nations **breached** the agreements and created new laws that took advantage of Indigenous peoples. Some countries have broken or violated every treaty signed with Indigenous nations. Today, countries including Canada, New Zealand, and Australia are seeking ways to reconcile with Indigenous people. This sometimes involves paying **reparations** for broken treaties.

KEY PLAYERS

In 1969, the Vienna Convention on the Law of Treaties was created. It set out rules for creating, changing, interpreting, ending, and resolving disputes around treaties. Today 113 countries have signed the Convention and agree to follow its rules.

▼ Some military alliances and treaties allow for units from one nation to train with stronger or more advanced nations. This helps all members become more capable of defending their territories.

▼ These Māori people of New Zealand mark Waitangi Day, which commemorates the 1840 Treaty of Waitangi. Considered the founding document of New Zealand, it was signed by representatives of the British Crown and more than 500 Māori chiefs. The treaty was written in English and Māori. Many people argue each has different meanings.

War and conflict can result in horrific loss of life as well as damage to **infrastructure**, the economy, and the landscape of areas involved. It is not surprising that after wars, countries form alliances to prevent similar conflicts from happening again. At the same time, preexisting alliances also played a role in how and why local conflicts became world wars.

WORLD WAR I ALLIANCES

Earlier wars in Europe in the 1800s created two large alliances: The Triple Alliance between Germany, Austria-Hungary, and Italy, and the Triple Entente, an agreement between Great Britain, France, and Russia. When Austrian Archduke Ferdinand was assassinated in 1914, Austria-Hungary declared war on Serbia.

Russia, which had an agreement with Serbia, came to its aid. As a result, Germany, which was tied to Austria-Hungary, declared war on Russia. The Triple Entente agreement meant Great Britain and France supported Russia against Germany. On and on, countries chose sides until more than 30 nations had declared war. World War I had begun. Five years later, the 1919 Treaty of Versailles set out the terms of the war's end.

▼ When the Lusitania, a British passenger ship, was sunk by a German submarine in 1915, media coverage resulted in public outrage against Germany. Some called for the United States to enter the war.

"All the News That's Fit to Print."

The New York Times.

EXTRA 5:30 A. M.

VOL. LXIV...NO. 20,923. NEW YORK, SATURDAY, MAY 8, 1915.—TWENTY-FOUR PAGES. ONE CENT

LUSITANIA SUNK BY A SUBMARINE, PROBABLY 1,260 DEAD; TWICE TORPEDOED OFF IRISH COAST; SINKS IN 15 MINUTES; CAPT. TURNER SAVED, FROHMAN AND VANDERBILT MISSING; WASHINGTON BELIEVES THAT A GRAVE CRISIS IS AT HAND

SHOCKS THE PRESIDENT

Washington Deeply Stirred by the Loss of American Lives.

BULLETINS AT WHITE HOUSE

Wilson Reads Them Closely, but Is Silent on the Nation's Course.

HINTS OF CONGRESS CALL

Loss of Lusitania Recalls Firm Tone of Our First Warning to Germany.

CAPITAL FULL OF RUMORS

Reports That Liner Was to be Sunk Were Heard Before Actual News Came.

Special to The New York Times.

SOME DEAD TAKEN ASHORE

Several Hundred Survivors at Queenstown and Kinsale.

STEWARD TELLS OF DISASTER

One Torpedo Crashes Into the Doomed Liner's Bow, Another Into the Engine Room.

SHIP LISTS OVER TO PORT

Makes It Impossible to Lower Many Boats, So Hundreds Must Have Gone Down.

ATTACKED IN BROAD DAY

Passengers at Luncheon—Warning Had Been Given by Germans Before the Ship Left New York.

Only 650 Were Saved,

▲ Austro-Hungarian prisoners of war are marched past advancing Russian troops during the **siege** of Przemyśl, Poland. At 133 days, it was the longest European siege during the war and was costly in lives and money.

▲ At the Paris Peace Conference (1919–1920), the victorious **Allies** determined that the Treaty of Versailles would place the responsibility for World War I entirely on Germany and its allies.

▶ The United States tried to avoid getting involved in WWI. However, as the conflict grew, events compelled the country to join its allies.

WORLD WAR II ALLIANCES

In the years leading up to WWII, Great Britain and France had formed an alliance with Poland to help protect it in case of invasion by Germany. When Germany invaded in September 1939, Great Britain and France declared war on Germany. Similar to WWI, other countries that had separate agreements took sides until many parts of the world were involved. The Axis powers were Germany, Italy, and Japan. The Allies were mainly Great Britain (and its independent colonies of Australia, Canada, New Zealand, and South Africa), France, the Soviet Union or USSR (Russia and 12 smaller **republics**), and the United States. WWII was finally ended with the Paris Peace Treaties. These treaties detailed the rules for the defeated countries to make reparations and go forward as independent countries.

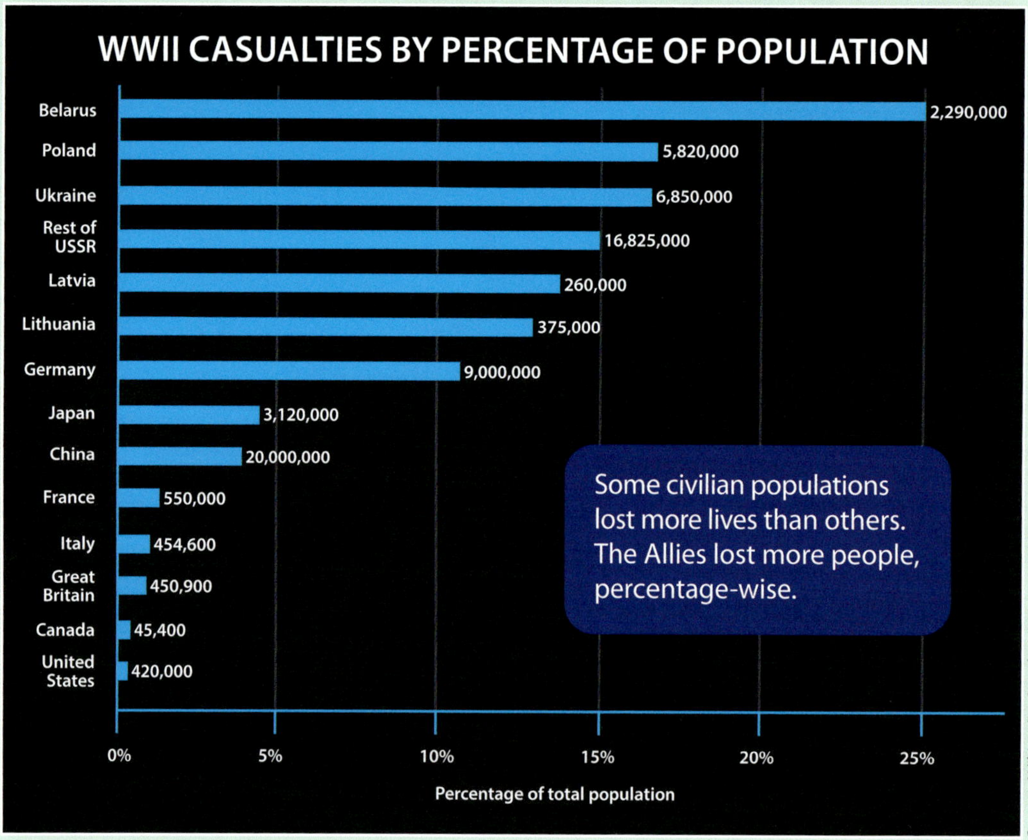

Source: Wikipedia, Randy Olson (randalolson.com/@randal_olson)

▲ The North Atlantic Treaty, or Washington Treaty, was signed by the 12 founding members of NATO in Washington, DC, on April 4, 1949. It laid out the guidelines for a mutual defense agreement and required that member countries share in values of **democracy**, human rights, and the rule of law.

World War II reminded countries of how important allies are during conflict. After the war, a number of new alliance organizations and treaties were made to help ensure peace through cooperation or mutual defense. Mutual defense is a pact in which members promise to defend each other in the event of an attack. Both the "West" and the "East" formed defense alliances. The West, or Western Bloc, refers to the **capitalist** countries in western Europe and North America. The East, or Eastern Bloc, refers to the **communist** countries in Eastern and Central Europe and Asia.

NATO PACT

The North Atlantic Treaty Organization (NATO) was created after WWII when Western Bloc nations banded together to support each other in the event of a threat or invasion. Its members agree to defend each other against attacks by third parties. The North Atlantic Treaty, which formed NATO in 1949, was originally intended as an alliance against the threat posed by the Soviet Union. The Soviet Union, or Union of Soviet Socialist Republics (USSR), was a communist-governed union of 15 republics in eastern Europe. It also had allies throughout the world. NATO began with 12 member nations during the Cold War (1945–1991), a period of heightened threats and tensions between the Blocs.

Today, NATO has 30 member states: 28 in Europe and 2 in North America. NATO's main headquarters are in Brussels, Belgium. It has its own military force with land, air, sea, and special forces units. Most of the time, they are **deployed** to help in the event of natural disasters such as earthquakes, tsunamis, and floods. In 2022, Finland and Sweden applied to enter because of concerns after Russia's invasion of Ukraine. NATO is considered the world's strongest and most powerful alliance.

The Warsaw Pact was the Soviet Union's response to the formation of NATO. It was signed by the Soviet Union and seven other Eastern Bloc nations in 1955. The Warsaw Pact worked to support communist countries and defend member states from any action by NATO. The Warsaw Pact began to unravel in 1989 when the Soviet Union started to break up. The Pact was officially **dissolved** in 1991. Almost immediately, Russia created the CSTO (Collective Security Treaty Organization) in 1992. It consists of Russia and five other Eastern European countries that were previously part of the Soviet Union. It is similar to NATO in that an attack against one is seen as an attack against all of them.

NORAD (North American Aerospace Defense Command) is an alliance between Canada and the U.S. created in 1958. It is a joint effort to protect North American aerospace. Technology forms a network of information and warning systems across the region.

▶ The Cuban Missile Crisis of 1962 was a 13-day period of intense threat to world peace. It began as a dispute between the United States, Cuba, and Cuba's ally—the Soviet Union—over Soviet missiles being installed in Cuba. Both the U.S. and Soviets were members of different alliances. Here, the Soviet ship ANESOV, loaded with missiles, is escorted away from Cuba after the U.S. and Soviet Union agreed to end the crisis.

NATO AND CSTO MEMBER COUNTRIES

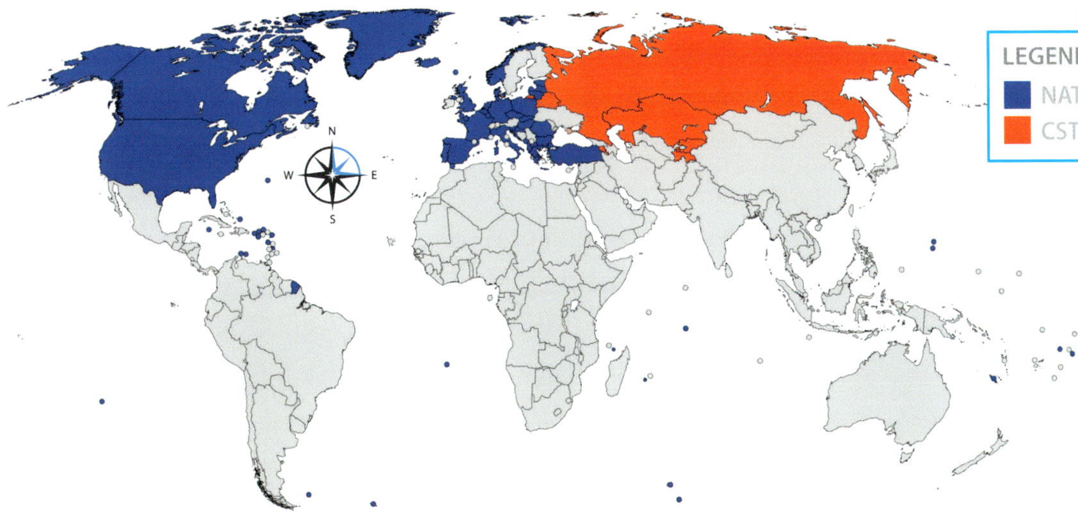

Source: Wikimedia Commons, Firdavs Kulolov

WHAT'S AT STAKE?

What are some new challenges international alliances might face because of melting Arctic and Antarctic navigation routes?

▶ The 9/11 attack was the first and only time NATO invoked its Article 5, which states an attack against any NATO member is an attack against all of its members. This highlights NATO's main aim: to defend its member states and their citizens.

THE UNITED NATIONS

The United Nations (UN) is the world's largest intergovernmental organization (IGO). IGOs are groups of countries that work together on issues of mutual interest. In the UN's case, those issues include peace, development, and human rights. The UN was formed after WWII with the goal of preventing future world wars. A total of 26 member states, or countries, signed the Declaration in 1945. Today, 193 countries are members of the UN.

▲ UN Peacekeeping is the collective responsibility of all UN member states and part of their UN agreement.

BLUE HELMETS

The UN has a peacekeeping force made up of military and police from member states. UN peacekeepers are sent on missions to prevent conflict, protect civilians, observe, and report on events. The Charter of the UN acts as a kind of treaty between countries. It requires all the countries that sign it to maintain international peace and security. Countries also must uphold international laws, create healthy lifestyles, provide human rights, and promote respect for all their citizens.

UN MEMBERSHIP

Countries must apply to become a member of the UN. They are first examined by the Security Council. This council maintains international peace and security. Once the Security Council recommends a new nation, the General Assembly has to vote to accept it. Some nations have not been admitted as members. Palestine has applied several times but has been denied. One reason given is that Palestine is not a recognized state—but 138 of the UN's 193 member states have recognized Palestine. Another reason given is the dispute between Palestine and UN member state Israel. Three UN member states—the United States, United Kingdom (UK), and France—have refused to allow Palestine to become a member until the dispute is resolved. A member nation that violates the principles of the UN can be **expelled**. However, this has never happened.

▲ The UN has received the Nobel Peace Prize 11 times.

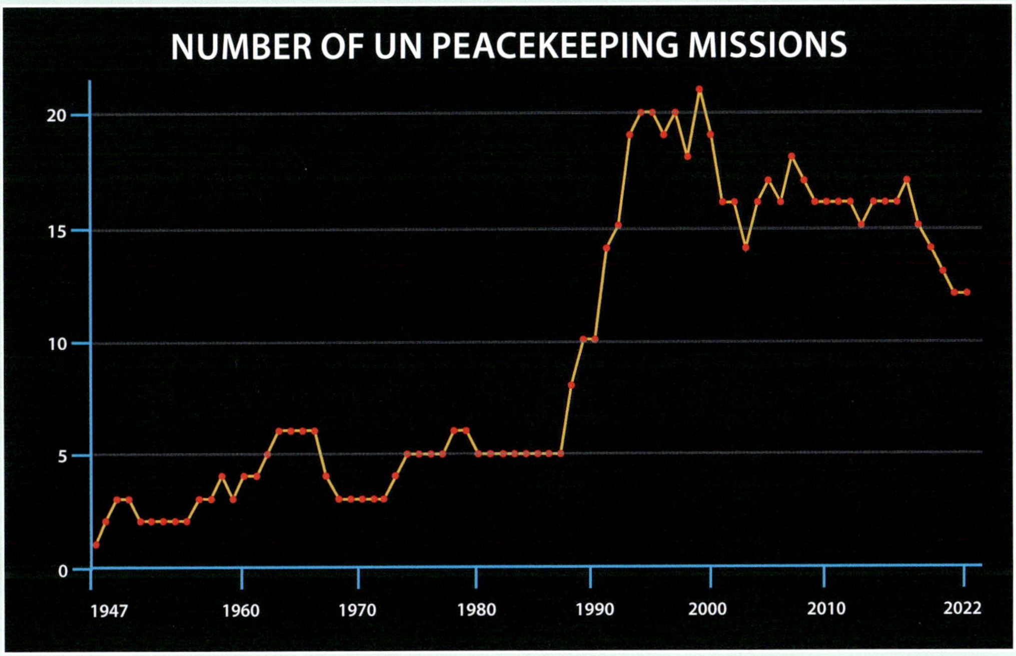

Source: Our World in Data

4 TRADE, HUMAN RIGHTS, ENVIRONMENT, AND SECURITY

Free trade agreements (FTAs) are intended to increase the wealth of all nations involved. They allow trade between nations without tariffs or restrictions. This allows a country to specialize in the goods it can produce and ensure that they can be sold for a profit. It then brings in other goods at a reasonable price for consumers. These agreements benefit the economies of all signing nations.

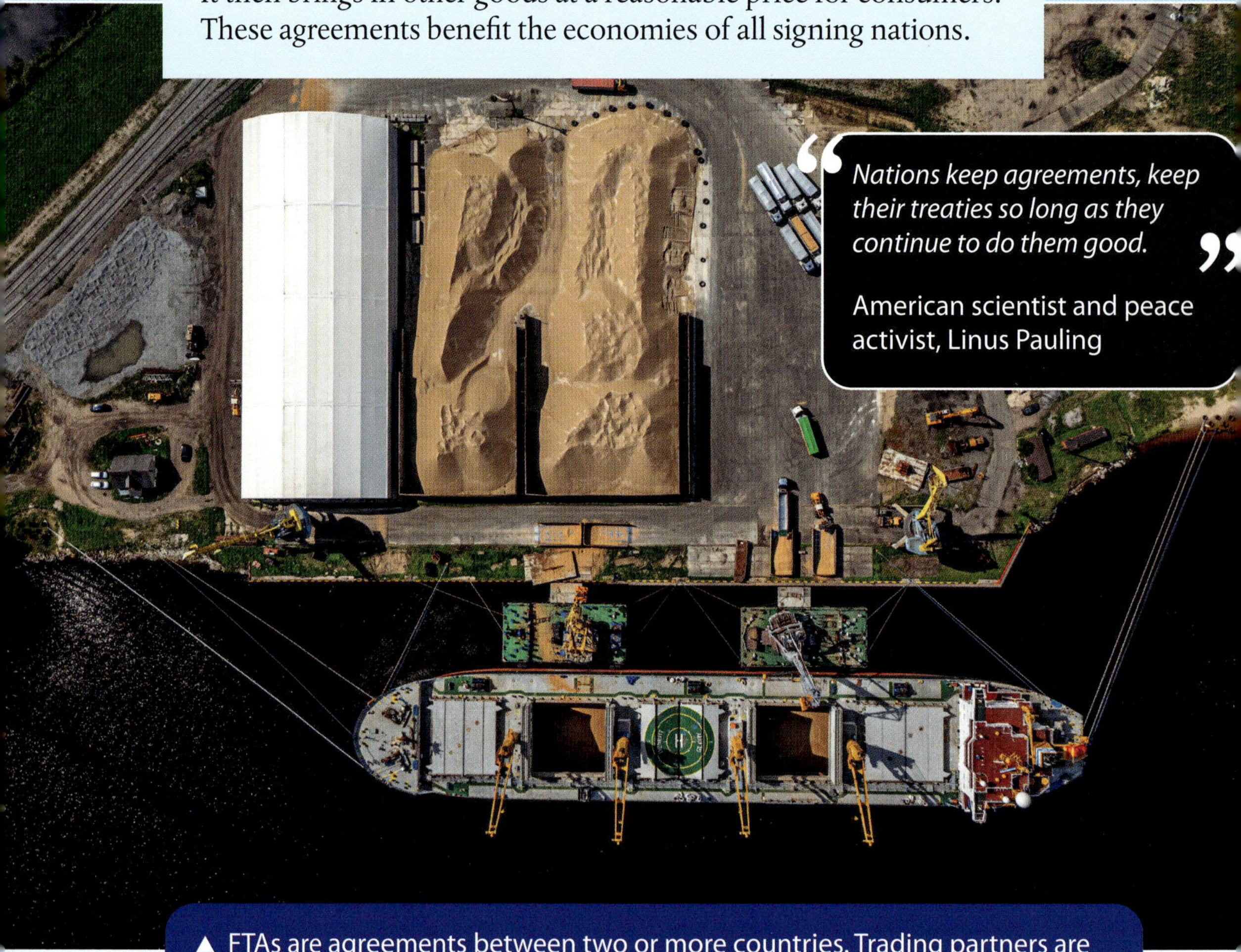

> *"Nations keep agreements, keep their treaties so long as they continue to do them good."*
>
> American scientist and peace activist, Linus Pauling

▲ FTAs are agreements between two or more countries. Trading partners are important to ensure that a country's goods can be sold without **arbitrary** rules or restrictions being imposed. Trade across borders feeds the world and brings products manufactured in one area to another area. Here, grain grown in one part of the world is loaded onto a ship for transport to another part of the world.

▲ Trade organization meetings and negotiations, like this WTO discussion, look much like other government meetings. Relationships and alliances are important for nations to get along and to continue trade.

LOW RISK HIGH RISK

WHAT'S AT STAKE?

What difficulties might a country and its people face if it doesn't join a free trade agreement?

TRADE AGREEMENTS

The World Trade Organization (WTO) is an international organization. It helps set the rules for trade agreements between its 164 member countries. It **monitors** the operation of these agreements. It also provides a place for treaty members to settle disputes.

The United States-Mexico-Canada Agreement (USMCA), also called the Canada-United States-Mexico Agreement (CUSMA) in Canada, is a regional free trade agreement between the three countries. It replaces the earlier North American Free Trade Agreement (NAFTA). The products most affected are auto parts, steel, aluminum, dairy, eggs, and poultry. It also includes environmental protections and increases the amount of **duty-free** U.S. goods that Canadians can buy online.

Other large regional free trade agreements are European Union (EU) and the Asia-Pacific Economic Cooperation (APEC). These treaties promote free trade across many countries. APEC is a group of 21 members, while the EU has 28. Since 1957, the EU has helped maintain peace across Europe. It also allows citizens of member countries the freedom to live, study, or work anywhere in the EU. Each country must treat EU **nationals** the same as their own citizens in terms of jobs, education, and taxes. All members use the same currency, which eliminates exchange fees when buying or selling goods. There are also no roaming charges for cell phones across all EU countries. The EU is also the world's largest **trade bloc**.

ENVIRONMENTAL TREATIES

The health of Earth's environment is a global responsibility. In order to protect plants, animals, air, water, and land, and to tackle environmental problems, countries have to work together. International environmental agreements are signed treaties that regulate human activity to protect our environment.

These treaties often focus on different areas of environmental protection. Species treaties focus on specific types of plants or animals, such as the Convention on Migratory Species (CMS). Habitat treaties, such as the International Coral Reef Initiative (ICRI), aim to protect **ecosystems**. Freshwater treaties are concerned with lakes and rivers, such as the Amazon Cooperation Treaty (ACT). Signed by eight South American countries, it aims to preserve the Amazon River basin. Energy, nuclear, pollution, and conflict treaties deal with such topics as controlling how power is generated and regulating how chemicals and poisons are used in the environment.

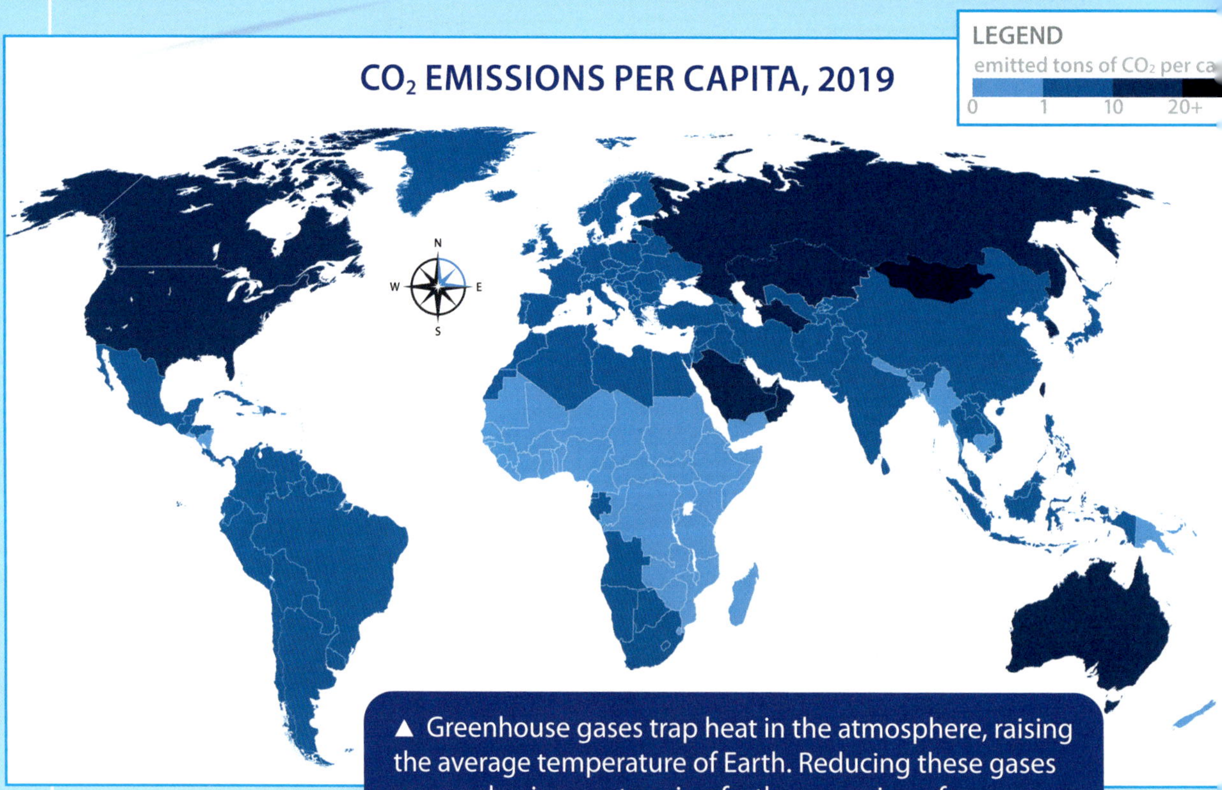

▲ Greenhouse gases trap heat in the atmosphere, raising the average temperature of Earth. Reducing these gases means slowing or stopping further warming of our planet. The Paris Agreement (see opposite page) requires countries to reduce their greenhouse gas **emissions**.

ENDANGERED SPECIES TREATIES

Nature treaties work to conserve and protect resources and systems. One is the Convention on International Trade in Endangered Species of Wild Flora and Fauna (CITES). This agreement protects nearly 39,000 plants and animals. It makes sure that international trade in wild species does not threaten their survival. Level 1 species are at extreme risk. Trade in these species, such as leatherback sea turtles, is banned.

CLIMATE TREATIES

Climate treaties are often in the news. These treaties are in place to tackle one of the biggest concerns we have in the world right now: climate change. The Paris Agreement is one of these treaties. There are 194 member countries. Its goal is to keep the rise of our global temperature well below 23.6 °F (2 °C). To do this, countries agree to submit action plans every five years that show their strategies to reduce greenhouse gas emissions.

▼ The Scarlet Macaw is native to Central and South America. Many were captured to be used as pets. Today, the Scarlet Macaw is on the CITES Level 1 list.

LOW RISK HIGH RISK

WHAT'S AT STAKE?

Some people argue that if every nation is not on board with solving global problems, treaties are useless. Do you agree with this? Why or why not?

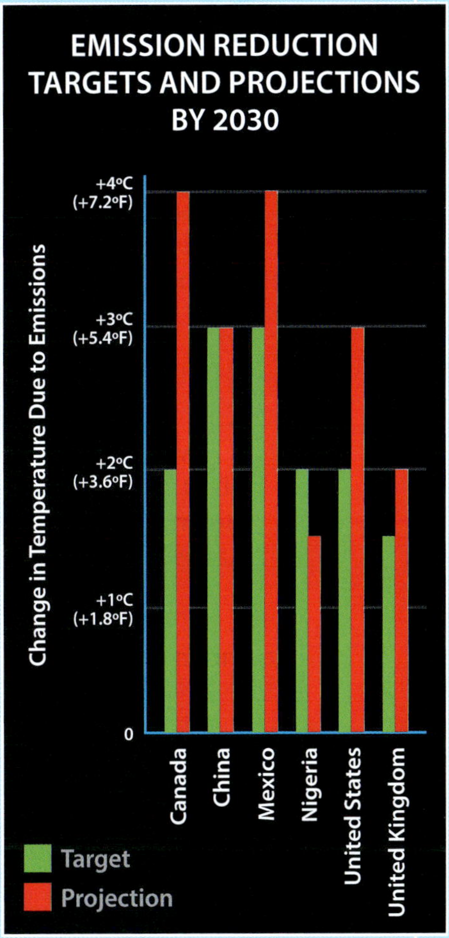

Source: Statista, 2021

Human rights are the basic rights and freedoms that belong to every person in the world, throughout their whole lives. These rights are the same for people of all backgrounds, religions, cultures, and regions of the world. However, not all humans live in areas where human rights are protected.

The United Nations created the Universal Declaration of Human Rights (UDHR) in 1948. It sets out the human rights that must be protected by all countries. The UDHR includes the right to freedom, justice, security, marriage, and freedom of expression. All 193 members of the UN have signed the UDHR.

REGIONS AND RIGHTS

Sometimes, human rights treaties are geared to certain regions. The African Charter on Human and Peoples' Rights was created to protect basic rights and freedoms in different countries on the continent of Africa. This agreement not only sets out the rights of Africans, but also their duties. These duties include responsibilities toward their family and society, and to preserve and strengthen positive African cultural values.

▼ In 2016, a UN tribunal found Bosnian Serb leader Radovan Karadžić guilty of **genocide** and **crimes against humanity** for his role in carrying out the **Srebrenica massacre** during the Bosnian War (1992–1995). He was sentenced to life in prison in 2019.

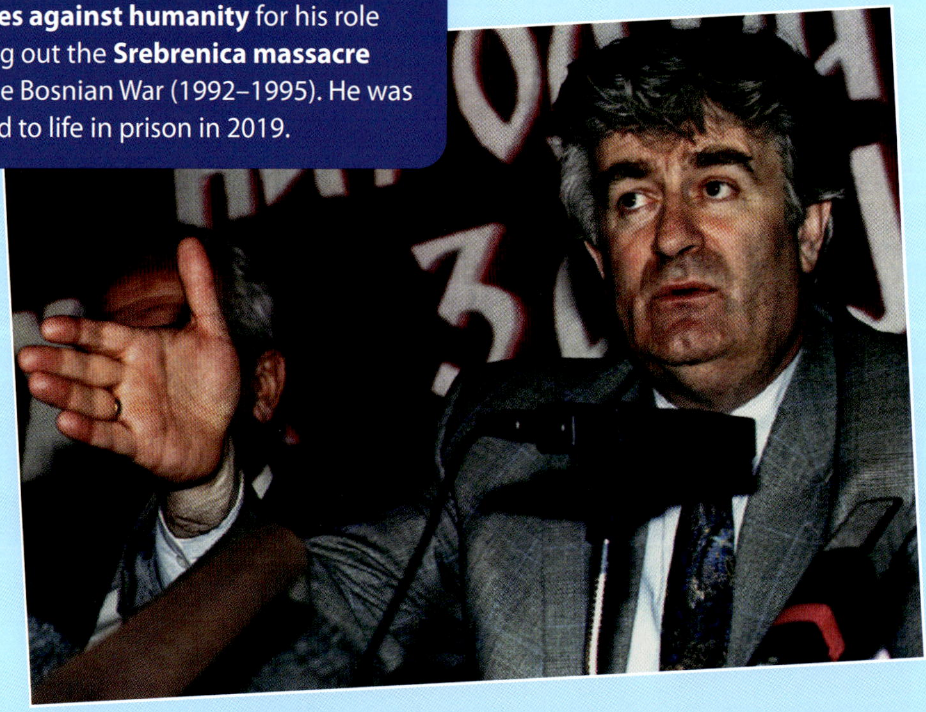

▼ In Warsaw, Poland, in 2020, people protested restrictions on women's rights. Human rights include not being **discriminated** against because of gender.

BANGKOK DECLARATION

Several leaders from Asian nations met in 1993 to create their own regional charter of human rights. Called the Bangkok Declaration on Human Rights, it states a commitment to the ideals of the UDHR. It adds that this document stresses economic, social, and cultural rights. Asian values include the idea of people working together for the good of everyone.

EFFECTIVENESS OF TREATIES

Some people argue whether human rights treaties are effective in preventing abuses. The majority of world countries have signed nine "core" human rights treaties, but abuses are still common. Some experts believe the solution is to make human rights laws stronger and make violators of those rights more accountable. Others believe that other solutions, such as providing economic help to struggling nations, will lead to fewer human rights violations. Human rights treaties and agreements have made a legal difference, however. Since 1945, many leaders of states have been charged in international courts for genocide and crimes against humanity. It takes a long time for these types of charges to be proven.

Violence and terrorism are threats faced by many countries. International alliances can provide governments with the information they need to keep their citizens safe. Around the world, countries have banded together to solve problems and reduce risks.

INTERPOL'S ROLE

The International Criminal Police Organization is known to the world as INTERPOL. Its job is to keep the world a safer place. To do this, the 195 member countries share information on crimes and criminals on a secure network. This allows INTERPOL to investigate crimes that cross international borders, such as drug smuggling, **human trafficking**, and **cybercrime**. They also help member countries prevent terrorist activities by identifying individuals and their networks.

OTHER SECURITY ALLIANCES

Other regions of the world have their own security alliances. The Arab League is an alliance of 22 countries in Western Asia and North, West, and East Africa. It promotes cooperation between member states. Its goal is to help countries remain independent and support the interests of the Arab world. It also supports economic ties between the countries and promotes peace in the region.

Five Eyes is an intelligence alliance between Australia, Canada, New Zealand, the United Kingdom, and the United States. It had its start during WWII when British and American code breakers worked together. Information is gathered from listening devices, online, satellites, and spies and shared with other alliance members. Today, the alliance uses its network to monitor terrorist activities and even war crimes in international conflicts. There are also other international intelligence alliances called Five Eyes Plus, Nine Eyes, and Fourteen Eyes.

KEY PLAYERS

Woodrow Wilson was a former U.S. president who witnessed the horrors of WWI. He imagined an organization that could resolve conflicts before they exploded into bloodshed and war. His idea influenced the founding of the League of Nations, which later became the United Nations.

Source: Wikimedia Commons, Master Uegly

▼ The Government Communications Headquarters (GCHQ) in the UK provides information for intelligence alliances. The UK shares its information with Five Eyes, Nine Eyes, and Fourteen Eyes.

Throughout history, country borders and territories have changed. Many alliances are created to help countries keep their independence and protect their form of government. Other alliances are formed to help bring about change for a better life for citizens.

ASK YOUR OWN QUESTIONS

In what ways could an online protest be more effective than an in-person march or protest? In what ways might it be less effective?

YOUTH AND ALLIANCES

The Milk Tea Alliance is an online movement by people in Hong Kong, Taiwan, Thailand, and Myanmar. It gets its name from the popular drink of the same name in the region. The alliance is made up mostly of youth activists who are protesting government overreach and pushing for democracy and human rights in their countries. The alliance started on social media, in response to Chinese **nationalists**. The alliance's influence is growing. Citizens of other countries, such as Philippines, India, Malaysia, Indonesia, Belarus, and Iran are also joining. It is giving a platform for younger generations to voice their opinions and act for change.

The Commonwealth of Independent States (CIS) was created after the dissolution of the Soviet Union. When the Soviet Union fell, several of its former republics decided to join together in the CIS alliance. The CIS provides a free trade zone and military defense. Member states also agree to promote and protect human rights.

The NAM, which stands for Non-aligned Movement, began after the Korean War in the 1950s. Many countries saw the world begin to divide into two major power blocs: those that were part of the Warsaw Pact and those that were part of NATO. Countries in Asia, Africa, and South America wanted to join together as a counterbalance to the two big blocs. There are 120 NAM member countries.

▼ Although the Milk Tea Alliance started online, in-person rallies, such as this one held in May 2021 in Los Angeles, also take place to raise awareness.

INTERNATIONAL ECONOMIC ALLIANCES

Trading goods is an important way for a country to increase its wealth and the standard of living for its citizens. By joining with other countries in an alliance, larger and better deals can be made to import or export products and resources.

Without tariffs or extra taxes on imported goods, trade agreements make items more **competitive** in price. This can increase sales and profits for businesses. This can also lead to more jobs and investment. With a bigger demand for products, factories can expand. It also gives countries access to a wider variety of goods and services than it can produce at home. The largest trading partners in the world are the EU, the U.S., and China.

U.S. ECONOMIC ALLIANCES

The United States has 14 free trade agreements with 20 different countries. With the EU, the U.S. exports products such as aerospace parts, mineral fuels, and machinery. It imports wine and beer, fruit and vegetables, and vegetable oil. With Southeast Asian nations it exports soybeans, cotton, wheat, and dairy products, and imports clothing and electrical machinery.

▼ When the UK left the European Union in 2020, citizens noticed a rise in food prices because the trade agreement had ended.

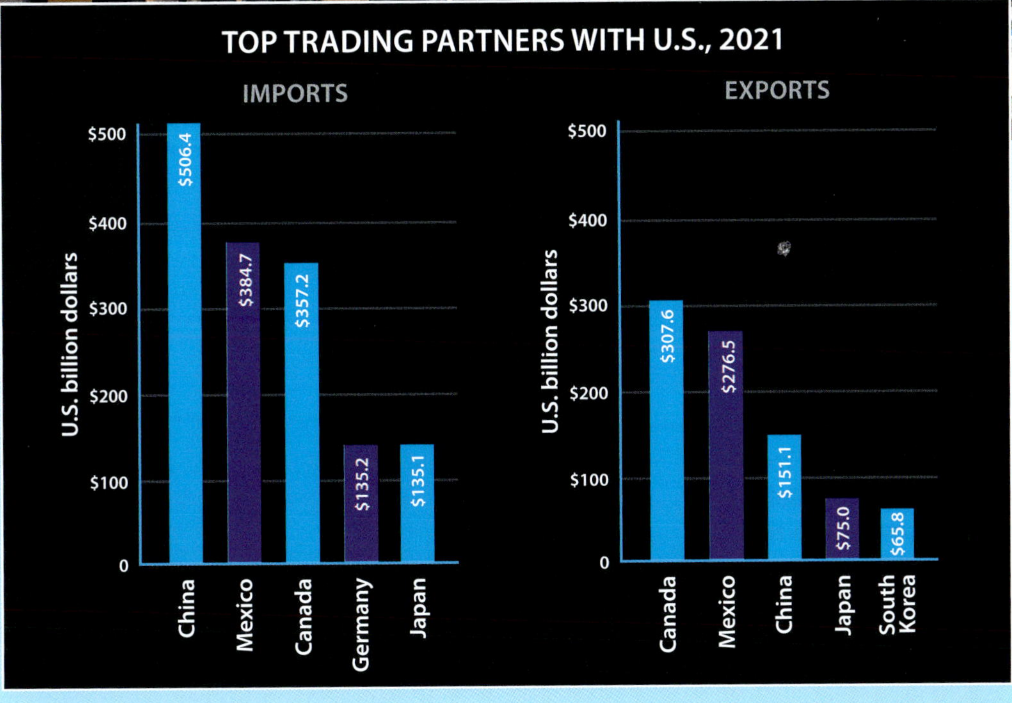

Source: Visual Capitalist, 2022, based on U.S. Census Bureau Report, Dec. 2021

CANADA'S TRADE ALLIANCES

Canada has entered 15 free trade agreements with other countries. Canada exports machinery, chemicals, and transportation equipment to the EU under the Comprehensive Economic and Trade Agreement (CETA). With Mexico, Canada exports such goods as plastics, minerals, and metals. It imports fruits and vegetables, electronics, and automobiles. With Australia, it exports aerospace equipment, electronics, and maple syrup, while it imports wine, medical goods, and minerals.

▲ Chrystia Freeland was Canada's minister of international trade from 2015–2017. She was part of the final CETA negotiations before the free trade agreement was signed in 2016.

AFRICAN ALLIANCES

There are eight trading blocs in Africa. One of these is the East African Community (EAC). It has seven member countries, including Kenya and Rwanda. The EAC imports many goods, including wheat, aircraft, and medical equipment from the U.S., and exports coffee, tea, nuts, and clothing. EAC countries have benefited from economic growth, improved **welfare**, and development of their industries.

5 WHERE THINGS STAND

As the world changes, so do international treaties and alliances. Different needs, resources, and threats will determine which nations should work together to share technology, markets, and military strength.

As we move away from fossil fuels for energy, new minerals and technology are needed. Nations that have the natural resources for technology will be sought after for trade alliances. Crops that contribute to **biofuels** will also be in demand. Materials needed to produce **renewable** energy equipment, such as solar panels, will also be in demand from countries working to switch to green energy production. Existing trade agreements for coal, oil, or gas might need to be reworked or shifted.

CHANGING LEADERS, CHANGING TIMES

Political systems may change with new world leaders. Citizens wanting to create a more open, fair, and free system could join together in an alliance similar to the Milk Tea Alliance. More voices mean more strength to create change. New governments can also lead to higher threats of violence or terrorism around the world. Security or intelligence alliances may shift as countries are added or removed to deal with new conflicts.

One example of this kind of shift is the change in the alliance between Australia, New Zealand, and the United States (ANZUS), which was a collective security agreement formed in 1951. In 2021, when New Zealand decided to pull out of the alliance because it disagreed with the use of nuclear-powered submarines, ANZUS changed to AUKUS. The new alliance includes Australia, the United Kingdom, and the United States.

> "*If the United Nations once admits that international disputes can be settled by using force, then we will have destroyed the foundation of the organization and our best hope of establishing a world order.*"
>
> Dwight D. Eisenhower, former president of the U.S.

PROPOSED CANZUK MEMBER COUNTRIES

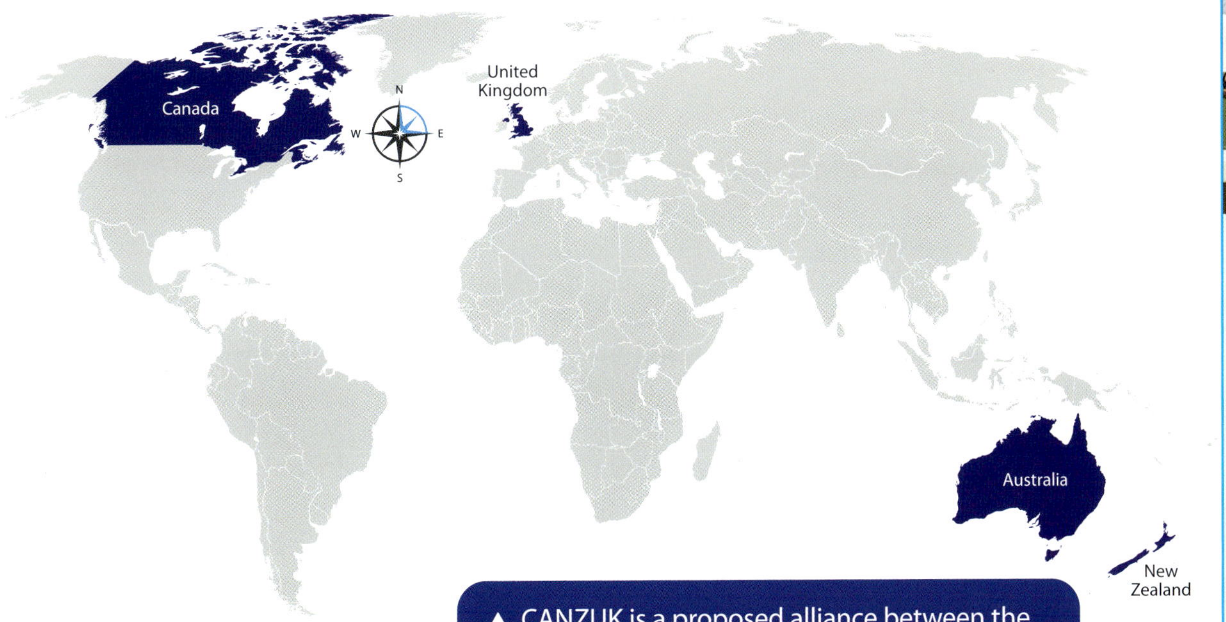

LEGEND

Proposed CANZUK Member Countries

▲ CANZUK is a proposed alliance between the four Commonwealth realms of Canada, Australia, the United Kingdom, and New Zealand. This alliance would focus on freedom of movement, free trade, and government cooperation.

▼ In 2015, Indian Prime Minister Narendra Modi proposed an initiative to promote solar energy as a strategy to reduce the use of fossil fuels. His idea, the International Solar Alliance (ISA) has now been signed by 110 countries. Many of the involved countries are in the areas of the world that get the most sunshine. The alliance aims to deliver clean energy to one billion people by 2030.

PROTESTS AGAINST ALLIANCES

Not everyone agrees with their country's treaties and alliances. Some people may not agree with the purpose of a treaty or alliance. Others might not support the other countries who are part of the agreement. Citizens might also feel that an agreement does not benefit their country as much as it benefits others. People can voice concerns and demand change in different ways. They can vote in new leaders and write to their government representatives. They can also organize and participate in protests and demonstrations.

Certain countries are sometimes seen in a negative light, due to world events. Some people protest U.S. involvement in international conflicts, for example. They are concerned with the power that the U.S. employs and may not support alliances with the country. Russia's invasion of Ukraine in 2022 brought a swift condemnation from many governments and businesses. This was a change from the almost nonexistent response to Russia's **annexation** of the Ukrainian territory of Crimea and part of the Donbas in 2014. Russia's involvement in international alliances, such as the UN, may be affected by its actions.

COUNTRIES' STANCE ON RUSSIAN INVASION OF UKRAINE

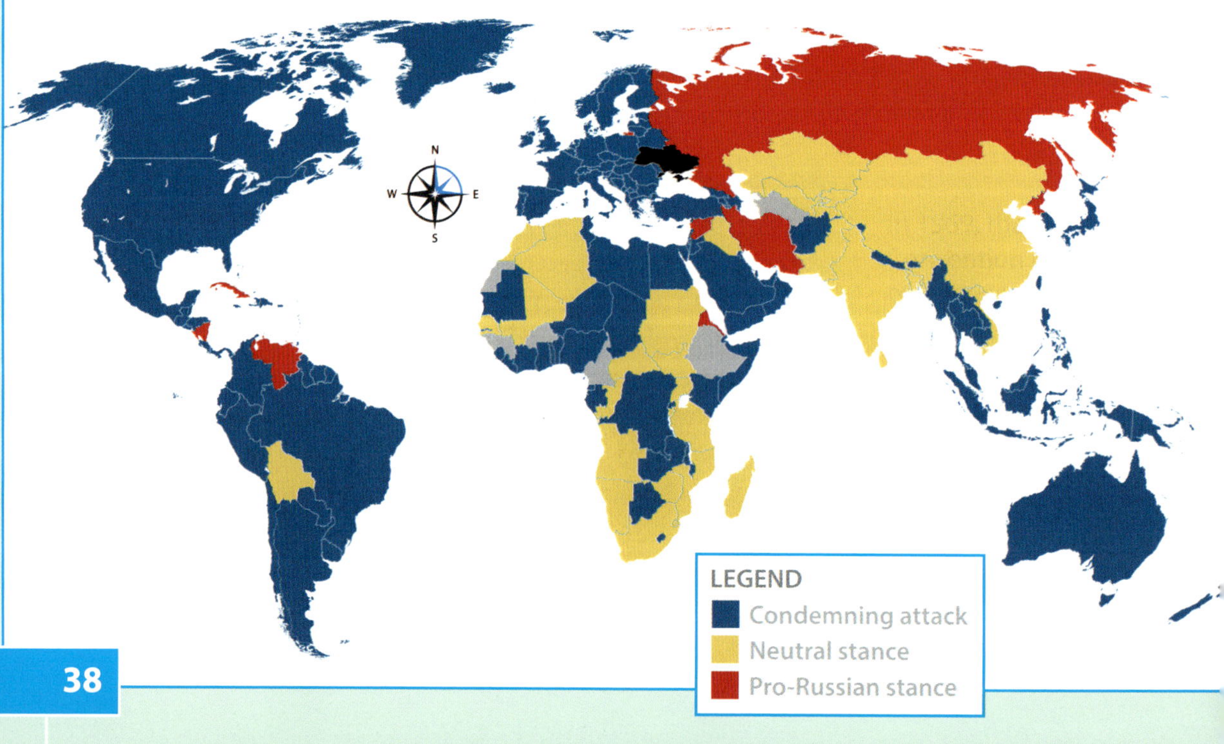

▲ Anti-war protesters in London, UK, hold up signs expressing displeasure with both Russia and NATO.

TRADE IMBALANCES

Trade between nations that do not produce the same amount of goods can create an imbalance. Countries with smaller economies may feel like they've been "bullied" into joining trade agreements. There is concern that people or businesses in these countries would not have the skills to take advantage of the opportunities brought about by trade agreements. In Guatemala and Costa Rica, many people protested the Central America-Dominican Republic Free Trade Agreement (CAFTA-DR) with the U.S. They felt the details of the agreement put them at a disadvantage.

The Paris Agreement on climate change has also caused disagreements between governments and citizens. Governments agree on the science behind climate change, but are divided on who is most responsible. It is also difficult for them to agree on how to set **emissions** goals. Some protestors demand even tighter restrictions on emissions. They say the current goals are not enough. Right now, even if countries reach their individual targets, the goal of keeping rising temperatures to 2.7 °F (1.5 °C) won't be met.

MYTHS DEBUNKED

Not everything we read is factual. It is important to consult reliable sources to research statements about international alliances and treaties.

Free trade agreements discourage businesses and people from buying local goods and services.

A free trade agreement usually does not require either government or non-government organizations to buy from trade partners. Businesses and individuals can buy goods from any supplier they choose. However, free trade does result in foreign products being more reasonably priced, making them more affordable to some.

The UN doesn't really do anything.

The UN feeds, shelters, vaccinates, and educates millions of people every day. UN efforts to vaccinate against smallpox has led to the disease being **eradicated**. It also provides billions of dollars needed in countries with **developing economies.** It has helped end conflicts and find peaceful resolutions in dozens of countries, including Cambodia, El Salvador, Guatemala, and Tajikistan.

The Paris Agreement won't help reduce climate change.

Some argue that because each nation sets its own goals, nothing will be accomplished. However, nations are required to revisit those goals every five years. Many countries that had never tried to reduce greenhouse gases are implementing strategies for the first time. Some progress has been made, but there is still work to be done to meet the goals in the agreement.

In a post-WWII world, there is no need for NATO.

In the beginning, NATO was created to oppose a communist threat, mainly the Soviet Union. It showed countries that they were stronger when they joined together. Today, the threats to democracy and freedom might have changed, but the alliance still provides collective security. By adapting to changing world conditions, NATO is still helping to keep member countries safe and secure.

ASK YOUR OWN QUESTIONS

What myths about international alliances have you come across? Where can you look for accurate information to fact check them?

▼ Since Russia's invasion of Ukraine, countries near to Russia's borders are nervous about their security. Recently, both Sweden and Finland have asked to join NATO.

6 KEEPING UP TO DATE

It is important to keep up to date on what is happening with international alliances and treaties because they are constantly being changed, expanded, ended, or created. The agreements made between countries affect all their citizens. Trade agreements bring new products into stores. Security alliances help keep people safe during conflict. Environmental agreements work to keep the planet healthy and tackle climate change.

It is also important to recognize that some alliances may not be positive for all. Some people point out that treaties or alliances can create an "us versus them" mentality. This can divide people and create the fear and mistrust that leads to discrimination. Countries that do not have trade agreements may experience more barriers when exporting and importing goods. Without security alliances, countries may also find themselves more vulnerable to conflicts.

▼ In 2021, the G7 countries committed to the Build Back Better World (B3W) initiative to help the world recover from the COVID-19 pandemic and address gaps in funding and infrastructure in climate, health, digital technology, and gender equity. Staying up to date can involve keeping track of the progress made on initiatives such as these.

> *"The twenty-first century will require a re-affirmation and re-definition of our alliances and international organizations."*
>
> Former U.S. Secretary of Defense, Chuck Hagel

WHAT'S AT STAKE?

In what ways can today's youth lend their voices either for or against international treaties and alliances?

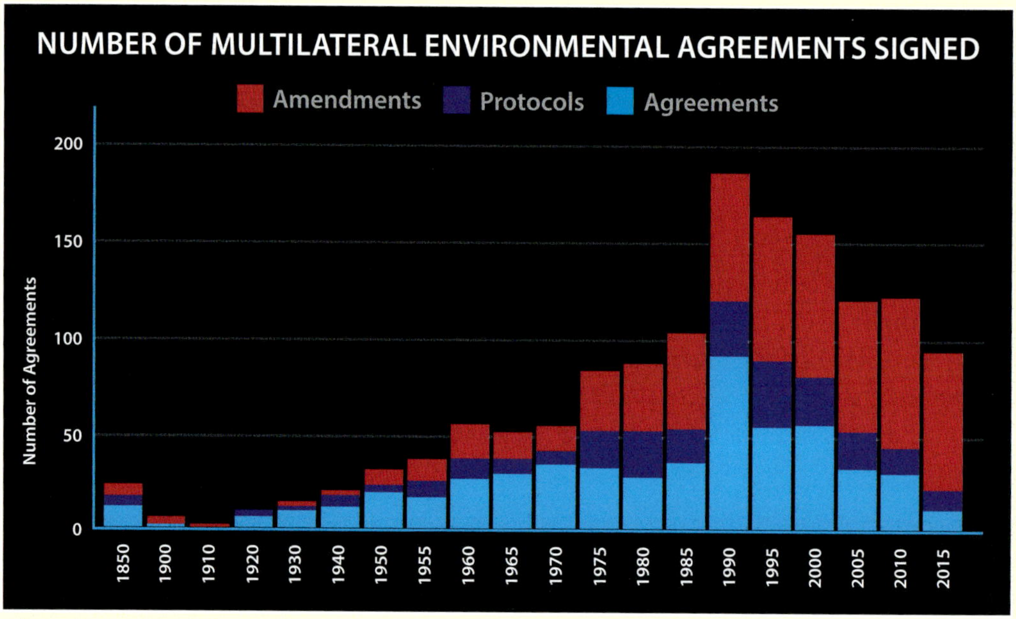

Source: Mitchell, Ronald B. 2021. International Environmental Agreements Database Project (Version 2021.1). Eugene, OR: University of Oregon. https://iea.uoregon.edu/ Graph generated on 1 Mar 2022.

TREATY'S TIME OUT

Most treaties and alliances are created for a set period of time. When the end date comes up, members can choose to renew it or let it expire. The Southeast Asia Treaty Organization (SEATO) was created after WWII to prevent the spread of communism into the region. Several of the member states weren't in the Southeast Asia region, but were concerned about the spread of communism around the world in general. Over time, member states thought the risk of communism was decreasing to the point that the alliance wasn't needed. SEATO was dissolved in 1977.

DELIVERING ON PROMISES

Sometimes, involvement in one treaty or alliance makes keeping promises in another agreement difficult. Since 1850, there have been more than 3,500 environmental treaties. These agreements range from lowering emissions to protecting diversity, reducing pollution, and slowing deforestation. Not all have been successful. Many have failed because governments also sign other agreements, such as economic alliances or trade agreements, that conflict with environmental goals. Knowing which agreements are in effect or under consideration can change decisions made by governments and citizens.

MAKE A PLAN

With international treaties and alliances affecting all parts of daily life, it is important to make a plan for how to stay up to date. Not all information is shared widely. Sometimes you have to do some digging and ask questions. By researching good sources and finding easy ways to read the latest news, you can stay informed.

One useful strategy is to set up online notifications for articles and news bulletins. Blogs, vlogs, and Google alerts can provide you with regular updates. Content aggregator sites also search the Internet for keywords or topics and collect them all into one place. This saves you the work of gathering information yourself. Some popular aggregator sites are Feedly, Panda, and Flipboard.

NEWS DIET CHECKUP

As with any research, it is important to audit your news diet. Auditing means checking your facts. For staying up to date, this includes checking how accurate and reliable your sources are and considering what bias different sources might have. It is important to have a balanced view. With the topic of international treaties and alliances, this might include viewpoints from different member nations of an alliance. It can also mean reading criticism or negative viewpoints to see if any points have merit. Blogs and vlogs are often one person's opinion or view and may be heavily biased. They can still be useful to read, but keep their bias in mind so you can focus on the facts. Other places to find up-to-date information on this topic could be statistics websites, journals, government publications, news magazines, or news programs.

SEARCH TIPS

In search windows on the Internet:

- Use quotation marks around a phrase to search for that exact combination of words (for example, "street harassment").

- Use the word Define and a colon to search for word definitions (for example, Define: gender equality).

- Use a colon and an extension to search a specific site (for example, Workplace sexual harassment:.gov for all government websites that mention sexual harassment in the workplace).

GLOSSARY

allies Groups providing help and support

Allies The name given to the alliance of countries, led by Great Britain, France, the U.S., and Soviet Union, that opposed Germany, Japan, and Italy in WWII

American Revolution The 1775–1783 war that led to U.S. independence from Great Britain

annexation The process by which one country forcibly takes over and proclaims ownership of another territory

arbitrary Uncontrolled; based on individual desires rather than reason

archives Collections of historical materials

artifacts Objects made by humans long ago

beneficial Favorable; having good results

biofuels Fuels made from living materials

breached Broken a rule, law, or agreement

capitalist Relating to the economic system in which private citizens own, produce, and sell goods for profit

colonization The process by which a country or empire settles and forcibly takes control of another area and its people

communist Relating to the economic and political system in which goods and resources are publicly owned and distributed, and workers are paid according to abilities and need

competitive Wanting to win or be more successful than others

credentials Qualifications that make someone suitable for a certain job

crimes against humanity Offenses in international law that involve deliberate attacks on non-military groups that cause human suffering or death

cybercrime Crimes carried out on computers or the Internet

democracy A system of government in which people participate in making laws through elected representatives

deployed Moved troops into position for military action

developing economies Economies that are less advanced, with less developed infrastructure and a lower income per person. Developing economies are often agriculture-based.

diplomatic relations The arrangements or relationships between countries, carried out by diplomats, or representatives

disarmament Reducing military forces and weapons

discarded Gotten rid of

discriminated Treated unjustly because of differences such as gender, ethnicity, and age

dissolved Closed down

duty-free Without added taxes

ecosystems Communities of living and nonliving things in a place

emissions Gas, heat, or light that is sent out into the air

envoys Messengers or representatives sent by government

eradicated Gotten rid of completely

expelled Forced to leave

genocide The deliberate and systemic killing of a whole group of people due to their nationality, ethnicity, religion, or race

human trafficking Forcing people to move and work against their will

Indigenous Relating to the first inhabitants of a place

infrastructure The systems and services that help a society operate, such as roads and power plants

monitors Watches the progress of something or someone

mutual benefit Both sides get some advantage

nationalists People who believe in nationalism, the support for a nation or region that stresses the importance of being "first" or "best"

nationals Citizens of a particular country

negotiated Dealt with an issue and arrived at a settlement

permanent Not changing

renewable Never runs out with use

reparations Payments made to those who have been wronged

republics Places ruled by elected leaders

siege A military operation in which armed forces surround a town or building, forcing those inside to surrender

Srebrenica massacre Also known as the Srebrenica genocide, the killing of more than 8,000 Bosnian Muslim boys and men

stakeholders People who have interest and are affected by issues, events, or decisions

strategic Carefully designed and planned

territory An area controlled by a country or ruler

terrorism Violence and threatening acts that seek to create fear and are carried out to achieve political aims

trade bloc Agreement between regions that controls trade and taxes

treaty A formal, legally binding agreement between two or more nations

welfare The health and wellness of a person or group

World War II The 1939–1945 war between the Axis powers (Germany, Italy, and Japan) and the Allies

SOURCE NOTES

QUOTATIONS

Page 4: Churchill, Winston: https://nyti.ms/3UT6SPB
Page 8: Ramaphosa, Cyril: https://bit.ly/3E1JybA
Page 14: Esper, Mark: https://bit.ly/3UWHKri
Page 24: Pauling, Linus: https://nyti.ms/3hL951q
Page 36: Eisenhower, Dwight: https://bit.ly/3EvJNx7
Page 41: Hagel, Chuck: www.quotetab.com/quotes/by-chuck-hagel

REFERENCES USED FOR THIS BOOK

Chapter 1: Why We Make Alliances, pp. 4–7
Cobden-Chevalier Treaty: bit.ly/3HMHKX0
Wars per pair of countries per year: bit.ly/3RnRLNm
NATO: bit.ly/3jgdHh8
Chapter 2: How to Get Informed, pp. 8–13
Abraham Accords: bit.ly/3Y8q9y8
Library of Congress: bit.ly/3kTXoa6
WIPO Treaty Terminology Glossary: www.wipo.int/wipolex/en/info/glossary.html
Chapter 3: International Treaties and Alliances, pp. 14–23
Government of Canada Treaties and Agreements: bit.ly/3WXKXHr
Harvard Kennedy School: Russia Matters: https://bit.ly/3jRvACZ
History: The League of Nations: https://bit.ly/3HHCEtU
Military Alliances of the World: https://bit.ly/3HKVT5L
NATO: bit.ly/3jgdHh8
UN Peacekeeping Missions: bit.ly/3jiVz62
Pew Research Center: bit.ly/3wQabNj
The United Nations: www.un.org/en
The Myth of Entangling Alliances: bit.ly/3HhEscS
US Department of State: bit.ly/3Dwa2T3
WWII Deaths per Country: bit.ly/3YjPbul
Chapter 4: Trade, Human Rights, Environment, and Security, pp. 24–35
ACT: bit.ly/3kO67ui
African Charter on Human and Peoples' Rights: bit.ly/3XTyUfA
CITES: https://cites.org/eng
CMS: https://www.cms.int/
European Union: bit.ly/3Jum6lg
Global Carbon Project: bit.ly/3Huz4U2
INTERPOL: bit.ly/3HmS5Yj
Statista—Emissions: bit.ly/3Y9dU4m
U.S. Trading Partners: bit.ly/3kZINex
USMCA: bit.ly/3DwVJxM
Chapter 5: Where Things Stand, pp. 36–40
AUKUS: bit.ly/3wOThi4
CAFTA-DR Protests: bit.ly/3JwN4ze
CANZUK: bit.ly/3JyP9KO
ISA: https://isolaralliance.org/
Statista: Response to Attack on Ukraine: bit.ly/40a5mMm
Chapter 6: Keeping Up to Date, pp. 41–43
Build Back Better World: bit.ly/3XXVyUf
Number of Multilateral Agreements: bit.ly/3Yf3G2C
SEATO: bit.ly/3wKuDPH

FIND OUT MORE

Finding good source material on the Internet can sometimes be a challenge. When analyzing how reliable the information is, consider these points:

- Who is the author of the page? Is it an expert in the field, or a person who experienced the event?

- Is the site well known and up to date? A page that has not been updated for several years probably has out-of-date information.

- Can you verify the facts with another site? Always double-check information.

- Have you checked all possible sites? Don't just look on the first page a search engine provides.

- Remember to try government sites and research papers.

- Have you recorded website addresses and names? Keep this data so you can backtrack later and verify the information you want to use.

WEBSITES

UNICEF helps explain the Paris Agreement and why it's important for youth:
www.unicef.org/lac/media/19316/file/paris-agreement-for-young-people.pdf

Learn more about treaties Canada and the U.S. made with Indigenous peoples:
https://www.thecanadianencyclopedia.ca/en/article/aboriginal-treaties
https://americanindian.si.edu/static/nationtonation/

Check out the UN website to learn about what the organization does and how you can help:
www.ungeneva.org/en/un-for-kids

BOOKS

Hollander, Barbara Gottfried. *Trade and Exchange*. Britannica Educational Publishing, 2019.

Minoglio, Andrea. *Our World Out of Balance*. Blue Dot Kids Press, 2021.

Sjonger, Rebecca. *UN Sustainable Development Goals series*. Crabtree Publishing, 2019.

ABOUT THE AUTHOR

Natalie Hyde has written more than 100 fiction and non-fiction books for young readers. She lives in a rural area with her husband and children.

INDEX